Lines Notes Life

Lines Notes Life: Another Solution
Copyright © 2022 by Pierre O. Henry

Published in the United States of America
ISBN Paperback: 978-1-959165-43-9
ISBN eBook: 978-1-959165-44-6

All rights reserved. No part of this publication may be reproduced, stored in a retrieval system or transmitted in any way by any means, electronic, mechanical, photocopy, recording or otherwise without the prior permission of the author except as provided by USA copyright law.

The opinions expressed by the author are not necessarily those of ReadersMagnet, LLC.

ReadersMagnet, LLC
10620 Treena Street, Suite 230 | San Diego, California, 92131 USA
1.619.354.2643 | www.readersmagnet.com

Book design copyright © 2022 by ReadersMagnet, LLC. All rights reserved.
Cover design by Ericka Obando
Interior design by Daniel Lopez

Lines Notes Life
Another Solution

Pierre O. Henry

ReadersMagnet, LLC

Another Solution

There has to be another solution
When I am faced with so many questions
My life and this community are two big problems
Dear God, I am asking you for the answers to solve them

How can I acquire satisfaction?
When I am lacking coordination
Is it a must to have good anticipation?
When in search of the right connection

I tired learning from my ancestors' revaluation
I often read to feel their true interpretation
I take pride in my education
Therefore, I practice my pronunciation

So I can one day put my knowledge into production
Now the time has come, but I am lacking motivation
Once again I am a step back, because
my mind is under rehabilitation
Furthermore, I'm distracted by these ladies; who are
all about seduction

Why am I constantly faced with a difficult decision?
God! Why is my life filled with so much corruption?
Sometimes I search for help in a deep meditation
Still! I cannot find the right combination

God Please! there has to be another solution
When I am faced with so many questions
I let you in, in the introduction
Now! Take a ride on the floating sensation

Why are blacks and whites organized in sections?
Why are the whites in control of all administration?
Why can't the world do the right thing and teach the children about appreciation
Sometimes I ponder; what would the world be like without segregation

Kind of leave a smile on my face, out of fascination
Back to actuality, I am in a shark attack situation
Though I know, I possess the right ambition
This world just will not give me its cooperation

Instead of facts, it proposes propositions
Lord! They do eat away at my determination
However, like the seasons clock I will forever function
To this world, I will provide timeless contributions

Simply! Like others I have thought about the next generation
True utilitarian, I present no discrimination
I believe where Just is due; there will be justification
Whether on you or me, or on any given nation

Dear lord! Show us another solution
Make it a repairperson; we are destroying your lovely creation

Simplicity

Come on dude... why try so hard
In these arms lady... life is hard
Steps are in places for a reason
Sounds make music for a reason
Sunday dinner with my family...
Simplicity
Listening to my son express
himself... Simplicity

Before we complete we have to start
Enjoying nature strengthens the
heart
A baby's first breath last forever
A new experience set life together
Inference means comprehend before
reacting
Acceptance means acknowledge before
acting
I enjoy watching day turn to night...
Simplicity

"Changes

New habits, same routine
New vision, same scene
Big vocabulary, same message
Different chapter, same passage
Change is about to come!

Bold stands, weak knees
Domestic dog, wild fleas
Deep meditation, free thoughts
United structure, loose parts
Change is about to come!

God advocate for love
God advocate for peace
God advocate for unity
God advocate for success
Change is about to come!

You get out, what you put in
You finish, what you begin
Mentally developed, physically accomplished
Prayers are prayed, destiny not a wish
Changes are about to come

Actuality

Our eyes are openly closed to life's reality
Ignoring faith living for destiny
Forecasting tomorrow, forgetting today
Disguising the commandments in order to play
In our society which creates our identity
Underestimating the actuality
Underestimating the actuality

Each breath prolongs our time
Another sun rise but no sunshine
Tears of a clown, leaves most Smokey
Turning nights to days, exposed internally
Now everyone can see our un-forbidden
Actuality! Is never forgiving
Actuality! Is never forgiving

Some buy dreams, others sell them
Some have solutions, others problems
Individually we all comprehend
Instinctively we all defend
Our characters in which we stand
Actuality, makes you that woman
Actuality, makes me this man

EMOTIONALLY LOVING YOU

The sun only come up when you open your eyes
Every minute with you I'm unwrapping a prize
My personal Cinderella without a magic shoe
Time apart only have me emotionally loving you

Our pillow talk is like everyday conversations
Our love is land preservation
Untainted, sincere like old country love
Emotionally loving you, my dove

Body language is stronger than the physical
Communication is truly spiritual
Supernatural, day and night I think of you
Everlasting, is me emotionally loving you

Who is the cornerstone, on which this love is built?
50/50 when we both share the guilt?
Understanding and
respect we are both individuals
Emotionally loving you is eternal

Lies

Lines Notes Life, the other solution
Understand the symptoms before taking the potion
Our needs should supersede our wants
Sun, water, dirt and time make trees out of plants

Killing means you are ready to be killed
Claiming a home you never helped build
It takes two to make this thing go wrong
If you were on your job, there would be no; so long

You jumped when the ship was going down
Why stay in a relationship, if it is not sound
Remember! We can see the ending in the beginning
Lines Notes Life, to whom are you lying

Living a soiled life, only turn sprites into ghosts
Haunting that which I enjoy the most

The Great Outdoors

I smile at the beauty of nature
Looking in your eyes ... I can see forever
Tramples on your surface are character traits
Gobble, Gobble; wild Turkeys in search of faith
Um... the taste of morning due
I am coming... the smell of Marsha's stew
Tropical like the rain forest when it pours
Like lost love, crying; The Great Outdoors
Like lost love, crying; The Great Outdoors

A broken down brown face... isolated
November... hunting season as slated
Red cheeked... she's an abandoned brick stone
Noisy creatures in and out they roam
Branches from a half dead pine, protects her pride
Most of those paintings should be gratified
Vultures' Pigeons' the sky they sore
The Concrete jungle, crumbling; The Great Outdoors
The Concrete jungle, crumbling; The Great Outdoors

John like candy... sandy be her feathers in Miami
Sunny Sunday afternoon at the Dolphins' game
There is no compromising natures' beauty
Humans... are the animals destroying your frame

Trying to make more out of more than you possess
Turning mental into financial progress
Time travels like water when minds explores
Moments captured, overwhelmingly; The Great Outdoors
Moments captured, overwhelmingly; The Great Outdoors

Honoring Dr. B

I am smiling; yes! It's all because of you
It only took one semester, for you to do what you do
Just in case you didn't know, you made me confident
You took your time and nurtured my strength

Now! I am that man I dreamt of
I am writing; something I humbly cannot get enough of
Your modest ways will not allow me to properly thank you
Where there is a will there's a way; I will show you I appreciate you

I am studying for life and I know I will pass
Smiling internally, you have already answered all the questions I needed to ask
Sure! My poetry will be about my writing style
I bet if you give an assignment; I will make you smile

Better yet! Pleased, to see that you got through
Dr. B once again, I am honoring you
I am putting so much time in; maybe I do need a break
You are in school every day; and you are my role model, for knowledge's sake

SLOW DOWN

It feels as though I am living in a fast car
I don't drink but I'm lounging at a sports bar
du-du-dum du-dumm duuu duummm da dumm
at times one plus one don't total two to some
du-du-dum du-dumm duuu duummm da dumm

Tracy your lyrics are like a bitter sweet plum
I am stirring, but still can't turn it back around
that's my heart not the bass making that sound
these dark clouds won't hoover much longer
my spirit is lighting up as the day gets brighter
du-du-dum du-dumm duuu duummm da dumm

at times one plus one don't total two to some
January 06 my confidence hit its lowest point
muscle relaxers won't free up these joints
with God leading the way I'm still breathing
ups and downs are determined by my setting
for me to get there, Lord you said to write
life's a journey, nothing happens overnight
du-du-dum du-dumm duuu duummm da dumm

This is the last weekend of the month
kicking off February, with no intentions of a punt
too many three-and-outs, with little progress
this time on the sidelines, my strategy I will reassess
du-du-dum du-dumm duuu duummm da dumm
there are times when one plus one does total two to some

Our Moment

"A thousand kisses from you is never enough"
Sincerely... my lips to your ears in ...our moment
I am never going to stop...ooooh my love
Longing like Luther...while enjoying ...our moment

From red to blonde highlights'...still utopia
As curled up emotions roll down your face
In your mothers' hallway on your birthday...Remember
So much was said with so little words...we gaze

I gave you the globe earrings... Promised more
A house on the hill and writing daily...feeling empty
I see your smile in all my triumph... I'm poor
Dian, Charles why didn't I chase destiny

But now I know...I'm in need of love... my moment
Congrats... Still nothing but love... your moment
What about us
On... On ... On... Our moment

Da Get Away

Bad day, can't wait to get home
Sugar! I am coming, cannot be alone
Walking my baby, my get away
Broke and stressed out, hey

Sure! You understand but can't comment
My hanker, as I live in constant movement
Life keeps passing me by, boats on the Hudson
Da get away, keep life from being so sudden

MIND OVER MATTER

Mrs. O says, it is like the blind leading the blind
Mr. P laughed at each line
Sara! You are here just for the money
Lance! She calls a black man honey

It is funny how decisions create the situations
Karma, decisions destroy occasions
Man! I am taking everything personal
Ghandi, doing right is universal

If you think I am not going to teach
These nuts, I live what I preach
Give me a moment and I will serve
I am not the best speller still my thoughts got nerve

Why our young black kids cannot see
This hood shit is destroying their Opportunity
Hey! That's what this community gets
Letting our kids run around like rejects

Disrespecting guards, teachers, administrators whoever
To them home don't mind, so actions don't matter
There is so much work to be done
These kids are not aware of what adulthood welcomes

Lord! Open the black community eyes
Those flashy things; are all a disguise
Black Gangs are just a form of slavery to the wise

Touching your Body

"Touch my body"; yeah, Mariah that's a hit
Lines Notes Life, every time Mr. H spit
Mood is mellow, Glenfiddich Special Reserve
Lost and stressed out with a stiffy curve

Can I see you? conversation on the phone
It's a cold spring night, and momma said I shouldn't be alone
"Go ahead, you will be alright"
See! I call in good spirits and you want to fight

"You got one thing on your mind, same story"
Is it wrong, because I want to touch your body?
Right there, love is love; no fear
leaving lips throbbing, baby I am Pierre

Lines notes life, read to relate
Spirits are flying; soul feels great
My arm on the back of the couch, she's in front
Jazz in the background, with emotions on the hunt

Peering in each other's eyes, while touching
Conversation is on point, time for loving
Easily, I compliment her posture
I am pleased to be in the company, of such mixture

You are classy, sexy and intelligent
Go ahead girl! Your father is a reverent
Blessed, by the man upstairs
Me in your life, you will never know tears

Do not take my love for granted, and play me for a clown
I carry a Glock 23, so I will hunt you down
Ooooooooh; I am inside from touching your body

YELLOW TONE BEAUTY

With curves that makes winding roads look silly
Skin so soft, it feels like a baby's booty
You should be the sun, the way you shine
Not fully developed, still I want to eat you

Green on top, bruised where you've been hit
Your birthmark reminds me of the great lakes
Thin line in the center
I am pleased with the exterior, longing for the interior

Tell me! Where are you from?
Can you satisfy my wants?
Sounds of a drum, when my hands slap your skin
It is you that make men act like men

Fresh! You have only been fondled
The thought of you make me dribble
I am longing to rip everything off
Then bite you where you are nice and soft

With that glow, you must be from Florida
You are too humble to be from hostile California
No more talking let us be on our way
It is your wet, juicy insides I will have my way

My Strength

My kindness is not my weakness... it's my strength
My kindness is not my weakness... it's my strength
My kindness is not my weakness... it's my strength
It's my Strength- it's my strength- it's my strength

I am a giver... Naturally
I do not deceive...I want you to be as happy as me
Hold up! You are not getting over
Take advantage and lose it forever

Goodbye Gerald Leveret... "Second time around"
Treasure this valuable... is the kings' crown
Respect- Appreciation... last a lifetime
Undermining ... is the worst crime

The love you lost... got you searching, searching all lengths
It's my strength- it's my strength- it's my strength
My kindness is not my weakness... it's my strength
My kindness is not my weakness... it's my strength
My kindness is not my weakness... it's my strength

I am not Gods' gift... thank you Planet Earth
However, I know just what I am worth
No one is perfect... but still
No one is a defect... why not power your will

Only friends can make you... who you are not
I am here to love you... and that's that
Because I care...doesn't mean I will sacrifice
Start taking advantage... will cost the greatest price
It's my Strength- it's my strength- it's my strength

Lessons in Love

I didn't write the book, I am still reading my pages
I understand, aspiration of life; This thing moves in stages
Also, it takes two; too deep, I'll leave that to the bees,
birds and now fairies
Also, these days; twelve and better are fulfilling sexual fantasies

Now! To explain the point, I am making
I'm too Foxx with it; so don't come hunting
I'm Sanford and son with it'; If I am not mistaken
I'm actually with it. Will you sacrifice for the lesson love got you
yearning?

Can you understand and respect enough, to enjoy our situation?
Are you mature enough to let love live, to fulfill your passion?
Or will you become dependent, I got your goodies in need of constant
stimulation?
Mmmmm! Time out, time out lessons in love should not be an
interrogation

I want to help you enjoy what you are afraid of:
see it with me.
Graced! With what others only dream of; I will set you free.
It's your body, mind and soul, I want to be more a part of; let that be.
Noooo! Too imperative; lessons in love should be more of a diplomacy

Red, red wine, and all of our first, should already be a sequel
You will pay! When I am acquitted at the trial
See, declaring victory in lessons in love, cockiness can be crucial
There cannot be our story if we don't model the script

Shed your shell, let me put that scent back in your shit
Alicia Keys the situation "I am asking you baby"
can my curve clog your split
I exclaim all lessons in love lead to us enjoying God greatest gift

Just words

They flow from her mouth without substance
lost in love she is looking for romance
Her sophisticated stride speaks to me
Buzzing for pollen she calls me honey
Just words, feelings have to flow

Shhh· she can't finish the sound
Awh- breathless she wants to get down
Mmm lips and eyes are closed
As the sun rises her love unfolds
Just words with no depth why so shallow?

Broken pieces of glass startles me
Open windows the wind talks to me
Sugar barks to say " I do care"
The birds sing 'ooo Pierre'
Just words i got substance not shallow
Whatever! you are a cool fellow

Just a Taste

This is Sunday morning conversation, Easy
An appetite for devotion, something tasty
Now! Let's get to the main course, nothing crazy
My passion is like a snow covered lake
So much inside, asleep or awake
I keep rebuilding on what others forsake
Just a taste, just a taste, just a taste

You light the fire, I will keep burning
I am not good at that; what? Misleading
I hate that, what? I'm a genuine
Humble like the bee, this is a blessed life
Not too much please, some don't understand a blessed life
Many don't know each breath breathe a blessed life
Just a taste, just a taste, just a taste

Some sing songs that makes no sense
Your ear should hear, only common sense
Don't misjudge the action many are overwhelmed
This is natural behavior, when you live overwhelmed
Every night he lays me down a happy man
Every morning he wakes me up a happy man
So; these actions they will never understand
Just a taste, just a taste, just a taste
Girl lick your finger this is too precious to waste

Welcome to America

Mae, let us start here if you don't mind
Before you open the door, let me let in some sunshine
Welcome to America

The land where freedom isn't altogether free
The land where pigmentation can determine your destiny
Welcome to America

Home of the brave, if you live in the white society
Home of the slave, if you confine your mentality
Welcome to America

Where your bank account expresses your persons
Where airwaves can make you a leader
Welcome to America

Knowing, objectivity passed away with mother Teresa
Understanding, subjectivity is the accepted culture
Welcome to America

The place where perception is not misleading
The place where words have no meaning
Welcome to America

If you acknowledge that the rules are subject to change
If you acknowledge that in-justification is not strange
Welcome to America

You will hear the slogan "black lives matters"
Then you will see young black men killing each other
Welcome to America

Here you are only wrong if you get caught
But even then, right can be bought
Welcome to America

Some are innocent until proven guilty
Some are guilty but damn they are wealthy
Welcome to America

Here connections, are a necessity
Then again connections can be a monstrosity
Welcome to America

Where friends are like the weather
And family, well don't expect no better
Welcome to America

Here children have no boundaries
And the parents crave the upper class societies
Welcome to America

Yes! Hospitals and clinics are the biggest drug spots
Yes! Corporations they call all the shots
Welcome to America

Now try to leave it better than you found it
But Don't forget first thing first, make sure you profit
Welcome to America

While police oversee the impoverished community
But they don't want the job, too much conformity
Welcome to America

Everyone has a dream to sell
Only a few don't already have one foot in hell
Welcome to America

Politicians are only concerned about what's taxable
As for doing right, they are not willing or able
Welcome to America

Hey the media facilitate what you see and hear
The media controls where you go and what you wear
Welcome to America

Veterans return home to get treated worse than most pets
However, once a year you hear let's celebrate our vets
Welcome to America

Where, what have you done for me lately is the motto
Where, private issues are now a reality show
Welcome to America

All people here are generational descendants
There are native Americans; but some whites are claiming that precedent
Welcome to America

Only if Jose could really see
How centuries have only thickened the hypocrisy
Welcome to America

Now try to leave it better than you found it
But don't forget first thing first, make sure you profit
Welcome to America

Running to God

I confess, the physical had me for 40 years
I confess, I heard you calling for the last 20 years
Though I answered, I never listened
No regrets, your understanding kept my blessings
In your grace, I will now reside
Running to God... With Jesus by my side

It's my commitment, which prolonged our bond
Living by your words, trying to walk on a pond
Without faith or true belief, I am sinking
Asking for forgiveness, thinking it relinquishes
sinning Closer to thee, I shall now abide
Running to God, with Jesus by my side

This is my testimony, as I seek eternal life
I rejoice with those, who in you they now take pride
No temptation can wane this declaration
I have strength in thee, to whom
I make this proclamation
You're faithful and just, I've seen with my own eyes
Therefore, I'm running to God with Jesus by my side.

Now I Know

I heard you calling and I didn't listen
You showed me the way and I didn't follow
You tried purifying my thoughts but I wanted instant gratification
Young and naive I had to learn the hard way
Now I know, lord you are the answer
Now I know, only you control the future
Now I know, lord we talk through my daily prayer

You rescued me from a life to destruction
You paved my path without any stipulation
Now I know lord you are the only solution
Therefore, your word is now my only protection
Now I know, lord you are the answer
Now I know, only you control the future
Now I know, lord we talk through my daily prayer

Your will is command so I shall always see the light
Forever your worker so I try to do right
I rejoice with those who glorify your name
Always in your presence is how my life is framed
Now I know, lord you are the answer
Now I know, only you control the future
Now I know, lord we talk through my daily prayer

You paved my path without any regression
So your word is now my only protection
Now I know lord you are the answer
You showed me the way and I didn't follow
Young and naive I had to learn the hard way
Now I know only you control the future
Your will is my command so I always see the light
Always in your presence is how my life is framed
Now I know lord we talk through my daily prayer

Happy Mother's Day

To a few mothers who deserves their day
Merry, may each moment be to You
How precious is a rose without its root?
Grounded, you stand in those responsible boots

Just a few thoughts to convey my notion
As for mother's, you are a great representation
Sending smiles to souls with the look in your eyes
Not understanding, you are first prize

Nurturing, which transcends all cultures
Pedals, embrace your future endeavors
The leaf, whom dictates to the wind
Angels, whom camouflages their wings

Enlightening, as a passage from God's verses
A gentle voice, which commands all praises
Like a chip in a cookie, you have fulfilled your duty
A mom to yours, but motherly to many

Not my Choice

I have drifted, it was not my choice
I have loved unconditionally, it was not my choice
I was pulled in, it was not choice
Who is to blame in life's lesson
How can you tell it is another session?

When can you tell it is time to take over
I no longer write my ending
Let go, let God; is my new understanding
I stood in sin, it was my choice
I walked in envy, it was my choice
I laid in lust, it was my choice
Why should I continue ignoring life's lesson?
Where will I encounter my next session

Now in faith I enjoy the journey
Let go, let God; thank you for saving me
All are called few choose
It is about grace not win or lose
What is to judge? They are your shoes
You are an example in life's lesson
Take notes during this session

Subconsciously all are suspicious
Let go, let God; time is precious
Gratefully I am content, it is my choice
Spiritually, eternally I breathe, it is my choice
Physically, I have to live it is not my choice

Good night my love

What is the matter with Jan?
Fighting her sleep, fun she cram
But, rock a bye baby; heavenly beauty
Already a mess, confident cutie

Please, Can I use your room?
Gracefully! The sun gives way the moon
As she turns in between, you are getting older
Fairytale or non-fiction you are getting smarter

Only good listeners become lifelong learners
Your garden on its best spring day; Janaya
The glow behind the sunlight, burning forever

Don't cry, soon I will be out of sight
Where is PJ, where is PJ in between each bite
Shower then to bed, each breath breathes a blessed life

Stressful Times

I am living under these stressful times
Under these stressful times
It's so hard to get over
Under these stressful times
All I do is live under stressful times
All these brothers are worrying about, what I'm stacking
I got all these sisters worrying about, who' I'm sexing
But, I'm just trying to live right, not stunting
Under these stressful times
Eyes closed meditating; I'm living confined
With thoughts clear as day, I'm searching a clouded mind
Under these stressful times
I am living Under these stressful times

It's so hard to get over
Under these stressful times
Letting someone in, leaves me susceptible
Fleeing the turmoil, heading for trouble
Knowing these days and times
Camouflage people sins,
I just want to stay in the race
No longer am I trying to win
Under these stressful times
I am living under stressful times
It's so hard to get over
Under these stressful times

It's so hard to get over
Under these stressful times
I got peace of mind within; still I'm living grim
I got all I need; however, I keep lusting
So much left to do, where do I start?
With the gospel in my soul, things are falling apart
Under these stressful times
I got one nostril out of the water
Trying to live life, without sinking further
Under these stressful times
It's hard to get over
Under these stressful times
All I do is live under these stressful times
It's everyman for themselves, under theses stressful times
All are worrying about wealth, not health
Under these stressful times
It's so hard to get over
Under these stressful times

Lola

My depth is vast like Tarry-Wild, with a low profile
Ooh child, hiking is making life a bit simpler
Pushing through Mother Nature, Pierre and Lola
Now she leads, barking for me to keep up
Her unconditional love, I can't get enough

Confidently strutin, friendly little somethin
Having strangers longin for her company
With a grin on my face, jealousy burns in my belly
Nawww!!! It's the fact that she's still in training
That's why I don't want other pettin and commanding

Lola, how did we embark on this mission?
Better yet, how did you become the key to my transformation?
Heaven sent, in a time of regression
The dawn of my evolution
Lola, the stimulation of my new vision

To Order Copies of

LINES NOTES LIFE
by Pierre O. Henry

Paperback: 978-1-959165-43-9
eBook: 978-1-959165-44-6

Order Online at:

www.amazon.com

www.readersmagnet.com/bookstore